LA GRANGE
PUBLIC LIBRARY

10 West Cossitt Avenue
La Grange, IL 60525
lagrangelibrary.org   708.215.3200

The Gruesome Truth About

The Egyptians

Written by

Jillian Powell

Illustrated by

Matt Buckingham

WINDMILL
BOOKS
New York

Published in 2011 by Windmill Books, LLC
303 Park Avenue South, Suite #1280, New York, NY 10010-3657

First Edition

Senior Editor: Claire Shanahan
Design Manager: Paul Cherrill
Designers: Fiona Grant, Jason Billin
Consultant: Anne Millard
Indexer: Cath Senker

Library of Congress Cataloging-in-Publication Data

Powell, Jillian.
 The Egyptians / by Jillian Powell. — 1st ed.
    p. cm. — (The gruesome truth about)
 Includes index.
 ISBN 978-1-61533-217-5 (library binding)
 1. Egypt—Civilization—To 332 B.C.—Juvenile literature.
I. Title.
 DT61.P695 2011
 932—dc22

                                        2010024573

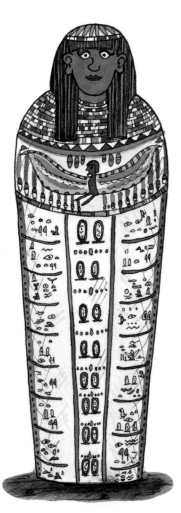

Manufactured in China

For more great fiction and nonfiction,
go to www.windmillbooks.com

CPSIA Compliance Information: Batch #WAW1102W: For Further Information
contact Windmill Books, New York, New York on 1-866-478-0556.

Contents

The Extraordinary Egyptians 4

Powerful Pharaohs 6

Pyramids and Peasants 8

A Slave's Life 10

Makeup and Wigs 12

Magic and Medicine 14

Hunting and Fishing 16

Gods and Gifts 18

Water and Worms 20

Criminal Punishments 22

Blood and Battles 24

Mummies 26

Glossary 30

Further Information
and Web Sites 31

Illustrator Note 31

Index 32

Answers 32

The Extraordinary Egyptians

The ancient Egyptians lived along the banks of the Nile River around 5,000 years ago. Ancient Egypt was a great civilization that lasted over 3,000 years. It was ruled by kings called **pharaohs** from about 3100 BCE.

The ancient Egyptians were skilled farmers, traders, soldiers, artists, **architects**, and **engineers**.

They built magnificent stone pyramids as grand tombs for their pharaohs.

▲ The Egyptians had their own way of writing called **hieroglyphs**.

▲ They learned to **embalm** dead bodies as **mummies** to preserve them.

▲ The pyramids are the oldest of the Seven Wonders of the World.

The Sun God

The Egyptians worshiped the sun god in the form of an insect called a **scarab**. Scarabs are dung beetles. The Egyptians thought Khepri rolled the sun across the sky each day, just as scarabs roll dung. They even wore **amulets** and jewels in the shape of scarabs.

▲ Scarabs roll and bury balls of animal dung so that the females can lay their eggs in them.

Those are some things that you probably already know about the Egyptians, but in this book, you'll find out the gory and grisly bits that no one ever tells you! Each double page will begin with a well-known FACT, before going on to tell you the **gruesome truth** about the Egyptians. Look for these features throughout the book—the answers are on page 32.

WHAT IS IT?
Guess the mystery object.

TRUE OR FALSE?
Decide if the statement is fact or fiction.

▶ The Egyptians believed in many gods that were part human, part animal, like Khepri.

Powerful Pharaohs

FACT Ancient Egypt was ruled by kings called pharaohs. They were thought of as gods.

Gruesome Truth

The pharaohs made Egypt richer by invading other lands and stealing their treasures.

Pharaohs and Pygmies

Narmer (about 3150 BCE) beheaded his enemies. He got his name "the Striking Catfish" from the Nile River fish that gives electric shocks!

Pepi II (about 2278–2218 BCE) sent an army to Africa and they brought him back a **pygmy** for his palace. Pepi was so excited by this "exotic" prisoner that he told his army to check him ten times a night on the boat back home.

Senusret III (1874–1855 BCE) fought the Nubians because they kept attacking Egypt. He kidnapped their women, killed their bulls, cut off their water supply, and burned their wheat.

Pharaohs had carvings of themselves made for temples, boasting about how many lions and wild bulls they had killed. On one hunt, Tuthmosis III (1479–1425 BCE) killed 120 elephants.

▲ One picture of Narmer shows him pulling a prisoner along by a rope through the nose!

▶ Slaves captured in war were the property of the pharaoh.

Fierce Feet

The soles of a pharaoh's sandals were sometimes decorated with drawings of his enemies, so he could crush them underfoot with every step!

Grave Goods

When a pharaoh died, his tomb was filled with everything he would need for the next life—even a toilet!

▲ Sandals decorated with the pharaoh's enemies were found in the tomb of the "Boy King" Tutankhamun (1334–1325 BCE).

▲ The first pharaohs may have had their servants and animals killed and buried with them. Later, they used models.

Pyramids and Peasants

FACT The pyramids are some of the greatest wonders of the ancient world.

Gruesome Truth

The pyramids were built by groups of peasants working long hours, with only one day off out of every ten.

Peasant Workers

Most people in ancient Egypt were peasants. They were sold with land and property, and were counted like cattle to show how rich the owner was. When the Nile River flooded farmland, they were sometimes sent to work on building a pyramid for the pharaoh. It took 25,000 men five years to build a pyramid.

Hard Labor

Some peasants did back-breaking work in the **quarries**, using hand tools to chip out huge blocks of stone. Others had to haul blocks weighing 132 pounds (60 kilograms) across the desert on sleds. Each pyramid took around two million blocks! Men lived in cramped, smelly huts with mud floors and got paid in food and linen.

Some workers got coughs and lung diseases from the sand. Others were stung by scorpions or broke bones in accidents. If they didn't work hard enough, they could be beaten, or even have a finger or toe chopped off.

8

▼ Men worked in groups of 20, heaving the stones into place.

TRUE OR FALSE?
Pyramid workers went on strike when they didn't get paid.

9

A Slave's Life

FACT Slaves in ancient Egypt worked as household servants and entertainers, such as dancers and acrobats.

Gruesome Truth

Some people were sold into slavery by their own families. Others sold themselves to escape debt, or were kidnapped from other countries or captured as prisoners of war.

▲ Sometimes, prisoners of war were **branded** or tattooed to show they were slaves.

Servants and Scarecrows

Slaves worked for pharaohs, **nobles**, or priests. They were often given as gifts or sold with land or property. They worked as house servants, on farms or in the mines.

Children were slaves, too. Some had to work as scarecrows in the fields!

▼ Children threw stones or waved their arms around to scare birds away from crops.

Room Service

Pharaohs owned thousands of slaves. In the royal household, each one had a different job to do.

▲ King Pepi II (2278–2218 BCE) kept some slaves naked and covered in honey, so they kept the flies away from him!

A Deadly Job

The worst work was being a slave in the gold and copper mines of Nubia and Sinai. If the slaves tried to run away, they were often captured and given a beating.

◄ In the mines and quarries, water was rationed and many slaves died from heat and exhaustion.

11

Makeup and Wigs

FACT Rich Egyptians wore makeup and wigs.

Gruesome Truth

▼ At parties, the rich wore cones of scented wax or animal fat that melted to perfume their wigs.

The best wigs were made from human hair. The wig maker had to comb out lice eggs before the wigs could be sold!

Cool Heads
Poorer wigs were made from wool or plant fibers. Many people, both men and women, shaved their heads for hygiene and to keep cool. Remedies for gray hair included ox blood, black snake fat, ravens' eggs, and rotten donkey liver!

▲ Mummified lice and lice eggs (nits) have been found on combs from Egyptian tombs.

▲ Pharaohs had their heads shaved because they were priests. They wore false beards made from wool or plant fibers—even female pharaohs!

Childhood Braids

Children had their heads shaved, too, except for a braid on the side of the head. It was cut off when they were about ten years old to show that their childhood was over.

Bathing and Beauty

Many people bathed in rivers or canals. They used soap made from ash and clay. Animal fat was used to soften the skin. To get rid of body hair, the ancient Egyptians used a paste made from crushed bird bones, oil, and tree gum. They also chewed gum from cedar trees to sweeten their breath.

Men and women wore makeup. It was made from mineral pigments mixed with animal fat. Some Egyptians also had their skin tattooed.

▲ Egyptian women used henna to color their lips and nails.

WHAT IS IT?

13

Magic and Medicine

FACT Egyptian doctors trained at special schools. They could stitch wounds and mend broken bones.

Gruesome Truth

The poor could not afford doctors. They turned to magic remedies to cure their problems.

Protective Amulets

Many Egyptians believed diseases could be caused by enemy spirits. They wore amulets to protect them against injuries and sicknesses.

Prayers and Remedies

Cures were often combined with magical spells or speeches. For eye problems, the Egyptians poured a mix of honey, red earth, and crushed pigs' eyes into the ear, while they said prayers to the gods. Sometimes, images of a god were drawn on a patient's skin. The patient licked them off to absorb their healing power.

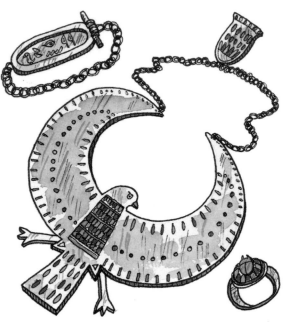

▲ Amulets, often in the form of birds and animals, were carried or worn as jewelry.

► For a toothache, a dead mouse was cut in half and placed on the patient's gums.

14

▲ For baldness, the Egyptians used a paste made from vipers' oil and bats' ears.

▼ One medicine was made from 19 kinds of pooh, from fly droppings to ostrich dung!

Mold and Maggots

Some doctors' cures did work, though. If a patient had a cut or wound, they cleaned it up with moldy bread and maggots, or they put raw meat on it and bandages covered in animal fat and honey. The mold and maggots killed the germs.

► For a broken nose, the doctor rolled up a tube of cloth, greased it, and pushed it into the nostril.

Hunting and Fishing

FACT The ancient Egyptians were skilled at hunting and fishing.

Gruesome Truth

They killed everything from lions, hippos, and elephants to hares, hedgehogs, and waterbirds. They killed ostriches for their feathers, and leopards and other big cats for their skins.

Birds and Bait
To kill wild birds, they used "throw sticks." These were wooden sticks like boomerangs that broke the bird's neck or wing, or knocked it out of the sky. Birds and fish were also caught in nets **baited** with grain or maggots.

▲ Animals were killed to provide meat or materials such as ivory and feathers.

To hunt crocodiles, the Egyptians hooked a pig's back and floated it in the river as bait. Then they made a piglet squeal on the riverbank to attract the crocodile. When it went for the pig, they reeled it in.

Hunting Chariots
Pharaohs hunted in chariots. Animals were sometimes herded into enclosures for the pharaoh to hunt.

▼ Pharaohs hunted with the help of dogs and tame cheetahs.

Hippo Hunts

Hippos were killed because they were a danger to boats and crops along the Nile. But hunting on the river could be a dangerous sport. The Nile contained poisonous catfish, as well as crocodiles. If a boat capsized, the hunters might become the prey!

▼ Hunters used lassoes to trap hippos, or speared them until they died.

▶ Hunting weapons included harpoons, spears, bows and arrows, ropes, and nets.

17

Gods and Gifts

FACT The Egyptians worshiped gods in temples, in shrines in their houses, and along the Nile River.

Gruesome Truth

They sacrificed animals and, at one time, enemy leaders of war to please the gods.

▲ The gods were even given makeup and mirrors as offerings.

Temple Tributes

The Egyptians worshiped hundreds of different gods and goddesses. They made offerings of food, drinks, and other gifts to statues of the gods in their temples.

Animal Offerings

Cattle, geese, **antelopes**, and **gazelles** were all sacrificed outside temples for the gods. Priests cut the animal's throat, then cut off its head before skinning it.

▼ After sacrifice, animal remains were sometimes thrown into the Nile River.

Tomb Companions

In the days of the first pharaohs, when the king died, his servants, **scribes**, and soldiers might be killed and buried with him. They were poisoned, strangled, or had their throats cut. His horses, camels, donkeys, dogs, and cats were also mummified and put in the tomb.

▼ One early pharaoh's tomb contained over 300 burials—thought to be his servants!

WHAT IS IT?

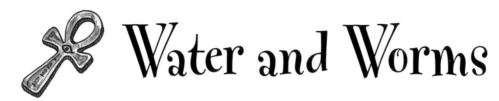

Water and Worms

FACT The Nile River flooded each year and provided the Egyptians with rich farmland.

Gruesome Truth

Nile water contained many kinds of **parasites**. When people waded in the **irrigation** channels, the parasites got into their legs and feet and laid eggs in their blood.

▲ Drinking water contained sewage because toilet waste was thrown into the river, into pits, or just out into the street.

Wormy Water
The Egyptians used water from the river and from wells for drinking, washing, and cooking. The water they drank often contained parasites called guinea worms. People often had upset stomachs because of the dirty water.

Rats and Cats

Rats carried fleas that caused diseases. Mice and rats often ate the grain in houses and grain stores. Many people kept cats or rubbed gazelle dung and **cat grease** around the doorways to try to keep rats and mice away.

River Bathing

Pharaohs and nobles had bathrooms where slaves poured water over them from behind a screen. But most people bathed in the river or in canals.

▲ The Egyptians shared their homes with many kinds of pests including rats, mice, and poisonous snakes.

▼ Bread was so hard and gritty it wore down teeth.

Dismal Diets

Bread was an important part of the Egyptian diet. It often contained sand and grit from the millstone that got mixed in with the wheat or barley. Many people drank wine and a lumpy kind of beer, and often got drunk at parties. Wall paintings show party guests vomiting, or being carried home after drinking too much.

21

Criminal Punishments

FACT Egyptian pharaohs enforced strict laws and punishments.

Gruesome Truth

Punishment for crimes included branding, beheading, mutilation, and burning alive.

Cruel Courts

Law officers took criminals to the pharaoh who decided their punishment in court. This was often a harsh **corporal** punishment, even for small crimes. If a weaver took a day off work, he was punished with 50 lashes of the whip on his back.

▼ If criminals were caught stealing animal hides, they were beaten with a hundred blows until they had five open wounds on their back.

◄ People who avoided taxes could have their nose or ears chopped off.

Grave Punishments

Many crimes were punished by death. If anyone stole cattle, he was **impaled** on a sharp stake. His body was lowered slowly onto the stake, until it went all the way through and killed him. Then his wife and children were forced into slavery.

▲ Killing or injuring a cat was punishable by death, because cats were sacred creatures to the Egyptians.

Deadly Decisions

The worst crimes of all were plotting against the pharaoh and grave robbing. Grave robbers didn't just steal tomb treasure—they unwrapped the mummy to get at jewels in the linen! If they were caught, they were tortured and then killed. The pharaoh decided whether they would be drowned, beheaded, or burned alive.

▼ Grave robbers sometimes bribed the tomb builders or guards.

23

Blood and Battles

FACT The Egyptians had a well-trained army that won land and treasures for the pharaoh.

Gruesome Truth

Soldiers chopped off the right hands of their enemies to take back and show how many people they had killed.

Prize Parts

They often cut bodies into pieces with axes and collected the body parts as trophies to present to the pharaoh. King Menephta returned with the penises of 1,300 Libyan soldiers after one battle! The remains of the bodies were left for vultures and other **scavengers**.

Chariots and Sieges

Some soldiers rode in chariots, firing spears and arrows at the enemy. They used towers and battering rams to fight their way into cities.

They also fought with swords, javelins, knives, and throwing sticks. Sometimes, they clubbed their enemies to death with **maces**.

WHAT IS IT?

▶ Carved tablets and wall paintings record battles and victories.

Mummies

FACT The ancient Egyptians learned the art of embalming dead bodies as mummies. They believed that spirits needed a home for the next life.

Gruesome Truth

They embalmed mummies in open-air tents because the smell was so bad.

Insides Out

First, they laid the dead body on a table and washed it with palm oil to make it smell nicer. Then, an embalmer, called a ripper-up, used a sharp flint knife to cut into the body and remove the insides, leaving only the heart.

◄ The liver, stomach, lungs, and guts were washed in palm oil and wrapped in linen, then put into **canopic jars**.

Salt and Sawdust

The brain was pulled through the nose using a wire with a hook on the end. The body was put in a bath of **natron** to dry it out. After 40 days, they stuffed it with sawdust, rags, or sand and sweet-smelling spices, and sewed it up. They rubbed palm oil into the skin to soften it. Sometimes, they made small cuts in the skin and stuffed them with mud or animal fat to pad out the body.

▼ Embalmers chiseled into the skull through the nose, then pulled out the brain bit by bit.

Spare Parts

The Egyptians thought that a body had to be whole to enjoy the next life, so they patched up any wounds with gazelle skin and replaced missing limbs with wooden ones. Embalmers tied on finger and toe nails to stop them from dropping off, but sometimes pieces of the body fell off or were eaten by jackals.

▲ They put false eyes or onions in the eye sockets and painted the face with makeup.

Linen Layers

The Egyptians bandaged the body in about 20 layers of linen. Some people saved up all their lives for their mummy linen. Sometimes, embalmers put amulets between the linen to act as lucky charms and added pads to round out the body shape. Then, they brushed the bandages with a sticky **resin**, which sometimes stuck to the coffin.

▼ There were often several coffins inside each other. Each was decorated with protective spells.

A mask was placed over the head and neck, then the mummy was placed in a coffin.

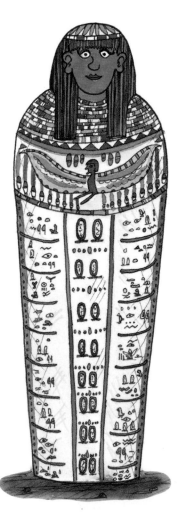

▼ The ancient Egyptians mummified fish, birds, mice, crocodiles, and snakes, as well as cats and dogs.

Mummy Pets

The Egyptians thought cats were sacred and important animals. They sold mummies of them outside temples. People bought them to leave as offerings to statues of the gods in temples. When a pharaoh died, the mummies of his pets were buried with him to keep him company in the next life.

▶ Fruit, animal legs, and other joints of meat were mummified as food for the dead.

 Glossary

amulet	A good luck charm worn to keep evil or sickness away.
antelope	An animal with hooves and horns, related to deer and goats.
architect	Someone who designs buildings.
baited	To set a trap with food.
brand	To mark on the skin by burning.
canopic jar	A jar or urn that contained the organs from embalmed bodies.
cat grease	Grease made from a cat's body fat.
corporal	Affecting the body.
embalm	To preserve a dead body.
engineer	Someone who designs and builds the working parts of engines, machines, or buildings.
gazelle	A small type of antelope.
hieroglyphs	A form of writing that uses pictures.
impale	To pierce all the way through.
irrigation	To water farm crops.
mace	A club made from wood with a stone or metal end.
mummy	A dead body preserved in sand or ice or by embalming.
natron	A kind of salt crystal.
noble	Someone from a rich or important family.
parasite	A creature that lives on a host animal.
pharaoh	An ancient Egyptian king or queen.
pygmy	A race of very small people from Africa.
quarry	A deep pit for digging stone.
resin	A sticky tree gum.
scarab	A kind of beetle.
scavenger	An animal that feeds on dead animals.
scribe	A writer or scholar.

Further Information and Web Sites

Books

Ancient Egypt: An Interactive History Adventure
by Heather Adamson
(Capstone Press, 2010)

Exploring the Ancient World: Ancient Egypt
by Jane Shuter
(Gareth Stevens Publishing, 2010)

History Opens Windows: The Ancient Egyptians
by Jane Shuter
(Heinemann-Raintree, 2007)

Web Sites

For Web resources related to the subject of this book, go to: http://www.windmillbooks.com/weblinks and select this book's title.

Places to Visit

The Oriental Institute Museum, University of Chicago, Chicago, IL

Museum of Fine Arts, Boston, MA

Freer & Sackler Galleries, Smithsonian Institution, Washington, DC

Illustrator Note

The ancient Egyptians have always fascinated me from the time I first learned about them at school. Their amazing buildings, artwork, and religion stand as a testament to time for us all to see. However, time has not forgotten the other side of Egyptian life, the ghastly, grisly bits not normally told. Through illustrating this book, I have learned that there are some terribly gruesome truths about the Egyptians, too.

Matt Buckingham

 # Index

Numbers in **bold** refer to illustrations.

animals **7**, 16, **16**, 17, **17**, 18, **18**, 19, 23, 29, **29**

bathing 13, 21
battles **24–5**

chariots 16, **16**, 24, **24–5**
children 10, **10**, 13
crime 22, **22**, 23, **23**

drinks 20, 21

embalming 26, **26**, **27**, 28, **28**

food 21, **21**

gods **5**, 6, 14, 18, 29

homes 21, **21**
hunting 16, **16**, 17, **17**

magic 14
makeup 13, **13**
medicine 14, **14**, 15, **15**
mines 11, **11**
mummies 4, **4**, 26–7, 28, **28**, 29, **29**

Nile River 4, 8, 17, **17**, 20

offerings 18, **18**, 29

parasites 20
peasants 8, **8**, 9, **9**
pharaohs 4, 6–7, **7**, 8, **12**, 16, **16**, 19, 22, 29
prisoners **6**, 10, **10**
punishment 8, 11, 22, **22**, 23, **23**
pyramids 4, **4**, 8, 9, **9**

religion 4, 5, 14, 18

shaving, head 12, 13
slaves 6, **6**, 10, **10**, 11, **11**, 23
soldiers 24, **24**, **25**

tattoos 13
tombs 7, **7**, 19, **19**, 23

water 20, **20**, 21
weapons 24, **24–5**
wigs 12, **12**
work 8, **8**, 9, **9**, 10, **10**, 11, **11**

Answers

Page 9 True or false? True. The first-ever workers' strike was by peasants working on a pyramid for Ramses III (1184–1153 BCE).

Page 13 What is it? A face cream pot in the shape of a mother duck.

Page 19 What is it? An ankh, the ancient Egyptian symbol of life, which only gods and pharaohs were allowed to carry.

Page 24 What is it? Medals shaped like gold flies were awarded for bravery in battle.